WING CHUN

WARNING

This book is presented only as a means of preserving a unique aspect of the heritage of the martial arts. Neither Ohara Publications nor the author makes any representation, warranty or guarantee that the techniques described or illustrated in this book will be safe or effective in any self-defense situation or otherwise. You may be injured if you apply or train in the techniques of self-defense illustrated in this book, and neither Ohara Publications nor the author is responsible for any such injury that may result. It is essential that you consult a physician regarding whether or not to attempt any technique described in this book. Specific self-defense responses illustrated in this book may not be justified in any particular situation in view of all of the circumstances or under the applicable federal, state or local law. Neither Ohara Publications nor the author makes any representation or warranty regarding the legality or appropriateness of any technique mentioned in this book.

WING CHUN

CHUN

KUNG-FU

Technical Editor
BRUCE LEE

BY J. YIMM LEE

BLACK BELT BOOKS
A Division of **OHARA** Ⓟ **PUBLICATIONS, INC.**
World Leader in Martial Arts Publications

DEDICATION

To my wife Kathy
R.I.P.

© Ohara Publications, Incorporated 1972
Printed in the United States of America
Library of Congress Catalog Card Number: 72-87863
Forty-eighth printing 2005

ISBN 0-89750-037-7

FOREWORD

Actually, this book was never meant for publication. I started out taking notes on wing chun in 1962 so I could teach kung-fu to my eight-year-old son when he became old enough. As my son grew older, however, his interest turned to tennis—not the martial arts. I was afraid that my years of note-taking had been wasted. Then I decided to write this book on wing chun in hopes that it would benefit aspiring martial artists.

Wing chun has made a big difference in my life. Before taking it up, I studied the sil lum style, which featured such forms as "A Dragon and Tiger in Conference" and "Nine Dragons at Sea." I wasted three and a half years performing kata. Not once during those years did I see the students spar. We were told that this type of training would eventually lead to deadly "internal strength." I realized later that the whole repertoire was just a time-killing tactic to collect the monthly fee.

In disgust, I quit practicing this particular sil lum style. Later, through my brother Bob, I was introduced to my future wing chun instructor, Bruce Lee. Because of my unfortunate past experience in sil lum, I really appreciated the simple and direct style of wing chun and its practical application. What you practice today, you can use today.

I was fortunate to be able to study under Bruce Lee and be his assistant instructor. When he was living in Oakland, we were in daily contact. He was always there to clear up any doubts I might have about his style of kung-fu, and I kept copious notes on the pertinent points and techniques.

There are many kung-fu schools in both Northern and Southern China, but the most famous are the wing chun, pa kua, northern praying mantis, eagle claw, tam tuie, ying yee, and monkey styles of the North, and the wing chun, southern praying mantis, dragon, white crane, choy lay fut, hung gar, and mot gar styles of the South.

I have students who are experienced in some of these schools, and in exchange for wing chun lessons, they've taught me their styles. Someday, I hope to have books published on some of these variations of defense and attack techniques.

Television and motion pictures have tremendously increased the amount of interest in the Chinese, Japanese, and Korean martial arts, and as a result schools are springing up throughout the United States. Some are good; some are inferior. At present there are many Chinese as well as non-Chinese who claim to be kung-fu instructors. Eventually, kung-fu schools will go through the same type of upheaval and turmoil that karate schools have gone through in past years. There will be the inevitable bickering, pettiness, and ruthless exploitation of the ignorant public by the unscrupulous.

I hope this book will give the layman a clear perspective of kung-fu so that in his quest for knowledge he will enroll in a good school. Those who use the book for home training may pick up some useful pointers. If **WING CHUN KUNG-FU** is helpful, then I'm glad I took the time to take notes.

J. Yimm Lee
Oakland, California

ABOUT
THE AUTHOR

James Yimm Lee, the youngest of three sons in a family of eight children, was born in Oakland, California in 1920. He has always been active in physical activity and participated in gymnastics and wrestling in high school. In 1938 he was a weight lifter for the Oakland YMCA team and held the lifting record in his weight division for Northern California. He has also been an amateur boxer.

While working as a welder in Hawaii during World War II, Lee studied judo. He also practiced sil lum kung-fu in San Francisco for three and a half years before studying wing chun and jeet kune do under Bruce Lee in 1962. Only two other instructors have been personally instructed by Bruce Lee: Take Kimura of Seattle, Washington, and Dan Inosanto of Carson, California.

"I wish I could have studied under Bruce Lee when I was 21," says Lee. "Unfortunately, I'm more than 20 years older than Bruce. Still, it's better to learn a realistic approach to the martial arts late than never at all."

James Lee, a widower since 1964, is the father of two sons and a daughter. When time allows, he teaches certain aspects of wing chun and, occasionally, jeet kune do to a small class of less than 10 students.

Lee is seriously thinking of opening a physical conditioning center for middle-aged businessmen. "Fighting skill is very seldom required; often never," he explains. "But health and conditioning benefit people every day of their lives."

ACKNOWLEDGEMENT

Sincere thanks to Ted Wong for his help in demonstrating the techniques.

CONTENTS

FOREWORD 5
ABOUT THE AUTHOR 7
THE YIN AND THE YANG IN KUNG-FU 10
A BRIEF HISTORY OF WING CHUN 13
STANCES 14
CENTERLINE THEORY 18
IMMOVABLE ELBOW 21
FOUR CORNERS 24
ECONOMY OF MOVEMENT 30
THEORY OF FACING 33
FOOTWORK 34
SIL-LIM-TAO 42
STRAIGHT PUNCH AND FINGER JAB 122
KICKS .128
SIMULTANEOUS ATTACK AND DEFENSE 140
CHI SAO .142
TRAPPING HANDS 148
PARRIES .160
DEFENDING THE INSIDE HIGH AND LOW GATES 170
DEFENDING THE OUTSIDE HIGH AND LOW GATES . . .190
ATTACKING THE INSIDE AND OUTSIDE GATES 200
TRAINING METHODS 216
    Circling-Wrist Exercise 217
    Exercises for Strengthening the Bridge 218
    Punching Exercises 220
CHINESE TERMINOLOGY IN KUNG-FU 221

THE YIN AND THE YANG .

Kung-fu is based on the principle of the yin and the yang, a pair of complementary and interdependent forces that act continuously in this universe. In the symbol, the yin and yang are two inter-locking parts of "one whole", each containing within its confines the qualities of the other. Yin can represent anything in the universe: negativeness, passiveness, gentleness, femaleness, moon, darkness, night. The other half of the circle, yang, can represent positiveness, activeness, firmness, maleness, sun, brightness, day.

The common mistake of most martial artists is to identify these two forces, yin and yang, as dualistic (soft style and firm style). But yin-yang co-exist as one inseparable force of an unceasing interplay of movement. They are neither cause nor effect but should be looked on as sound and echo, light and shadow. If yin

. . . . . . IN KUNG-FU

and yang are viewed as two separate entities, realization of the ultimate reality of kung-fu won't be achieved.

In reality, things are whole and cannot be separated into two parts. When I say the heat makes me perspire, the heat and perspiring are just one process because they are co-existent—the one could not exist but for the other. If a person riding a bicycle wishes to go somewhere, he cannot pump on both pedals at the same time. In order to go forward, he has to pump on one pedal and release the other. So the movement of going forward requires this "oneness" of pumping and releasing.

Firmness is concealed in softness and softness in firmness. Activity includes inactivity and inactivity includes activity. This is what the black and white in the figure are meant to represent.

嚴鏡海徒孫惠亭

師公葉問贈

Mr. Yip Man of Hong Kong, renowned leader of the wing chun style. May his tribe increase.

A BRIEF HISTORY OF WING CHUN

According to legend, wing chun (literally, "beautiful spring-time") was founded by a woman, Yim Wing Chun, some four hundred years ago. Yim Wing Chun learned her basic self-defense from a Buddhist nun, Ng Mui, (nuns were quite active in the arts at various periods, and some were supposed to have been fierce fighters) and passed the style down through the centuries to Leong Bok Sul, Wong Wah Bo, Leong Yee Tai, Leong Jon, Chan Wah Soon, Yip Man (the present leader of the wing chun style), Leong Sheong and Wong Soon Sum.

Although Yim Wing Chun learned from another, she is still considered the founder of the wing chun system. She felt that too much emphasis was placed on the "hard horse" and "hard style" so evident in the other systems, and being a woman, she believed that a wiser course of action should be taken to compliment the "hard" way. In order to apply energy more efficiently, she devised the chi sao practice, a unique feature of the wing chun style in which one *flows* with the opponent instead of trying to dominate him (explained in detail in the chapter on the sticking hand). Since structurally this style compliments opponent strength rather than trying to dominate it, wing chun is ideal for women. It is an aggressive style with very compact, economical attacks and defenses.

Yip Man, the foremost authority of the wing chun art today, is responsible for bringing the style from behind the bamboo curtain to Hong Kong.

STANCES

Right Square Stance

To assume the square stance, distribute your weight equally on both feet and bend your knees. Position your hands at the centerline (joan sien), placing your right hand forward of the left.

Remain in the square stance, but place your left hand forward of the right hand.

Left Square Stance

Right Stance

To assume a right stance from the square stance, move your right leg forward, but distribute most of your weight on the rear leg. Continue to guard the centerline.

The left stance is the reverse of the right stance.

Left Stance

Right Sitting Horse Stance

From the square stance assume the right sitting horse stance (jor mah) by turning your body toward the right. Keep most of your weight on the rear foot. Lower your left hand, turn your palm toward the floor, and bring it across your body until it is in line with the right hand.

The left sitting horse is just the opposite.

Left Sitting Horse Stance

CENTERLINE THEORY

The centerline (joan sien) is an integral part of the wing chun style of kung-fu. It is the nucleus on which the defenses and attacks of wing chun are based. The centerline influence can be seen in all wing chun stances, hand positions, shifting of horses, advancing and retreating.

(A) In a square facing stance place your right hand forward and your left hand at the center of your chest. (B) When you change the position of your hands, regardless of the stance, never leave the centerline unprotected.

This series illustrates how to guard the centerline during the execution of several jabs in a training exercise. Start the finger jab from the middle of your chest so the jab protects the centerline as it travels forward. (1) From the completed left finger jab position, (2) begin a right finger jab by retracting your left hand as you shoot out your right hand. (3) Continue to move your right hand forward and your left hand back. (4) When your right hand is fully extended and your left hand is in front of your sternum, the right finger jab is completed.

(5) In a left stance place your left hand forward to cover the center-line. (6) In the right stance the right hand is forward.

IMMOVABLE ELBOW

The immovable elbow theory *(but doan jiang)* is very important in wing chun. Theoretically, it works like a hurricane. The eye of a hurricane is always still, but its periphery is constantly moving and exerting tremendous force. The immovable elbow works similarly. The hand and forearm can move in any direction, but the elbow never moves. It remains about three inches in front of the body. Also, the hand and forearm should never pass the imaginary perpendicular line that intersects the elbow. If the arm is pressed too hard, it is better to give way with the whole body than to give way with the elbow or violate the boundary line. The distance between the thumb and little finger on the left hand is the correct distance that the elbow should be from the body.

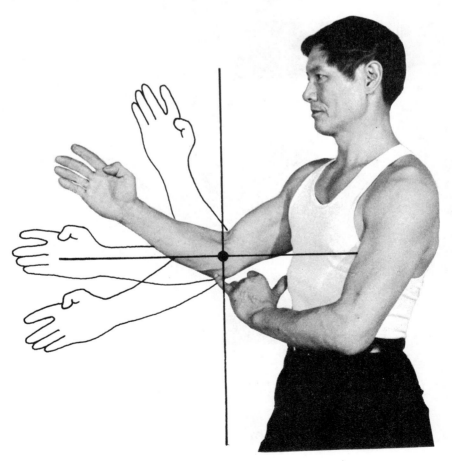

(1) The elbow is much too close to the body in this position. (2) In this position the arm is extended too much, making the body unbalanced.

In the immovable elbow theory, boundary lines limit the sideward and up-and-down movement of the hand and forearm. The height of the boundary is the eyebrows, and the lowest boundary line is the groin area, although the elbow must never dip below the navel. The width of the boundary extends just past the shoulders.

FOUR CORNERS

OUTSIDE HIGH GATE   INSIDE HIGH GATE

OUTSIDE LOW GATE   INSIDE LOW GATE

The boundaries of the four corners are the same as those of the immovable elbow: the eyebrows at the top, the groin area at the bottom, and the area just past the shoulders on either side. The four corners are divided into four equal areas, or gates. For instance, the top half of the side of the forward hand is the outside high gate. Any attack to this gate will be blocked to the

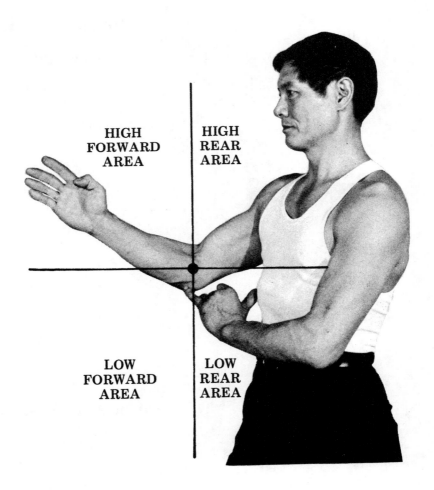

HIGH
FORWARD
AREA

HIGH
REAR
AREA

LOW
FORWARD
AREA

LOW
REAR
AREA

outside. Attacks to the inside gate will be blocked inward.

Within each gate there are also two separate areas as seen in the side view: a forward area and a rear area. Any attack to the forward area will be blocked by the forward arm. Attacks to the rear area will be handled by the hand that is back.

Outside High
Forward

This is an example of a forward, outside high block with the right hand. Note: One hand is high and the other is low.

Outside High
Rear

Here is a rear, outside high block (slap block) executed with the left hand.

Inside High Forward

An example of the forward, high inside gate block is the left palm-up block.

Inside High Rear

A rear, inside high block can be performed with a right slap block and a left straight punch.

Outside Low Forward

A forward, outside low block can be accomplished by executing a low, outer wrist block with the right hand.

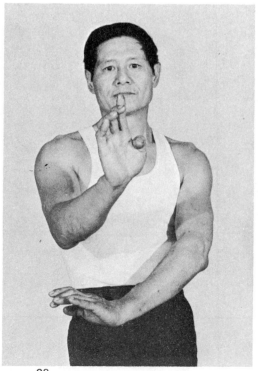

Outside Low Rear

The rear, outside low block can be executed with a low, left slap block.

Inside Low
Forward

The forward, inside low block
can be accomplished with a right
slap block.

Inside Low
Rear

A rear, inside low block is executed with a left slap block.

ECONOMY
OF
MOVEMENT

Practicing economy of movements in both defense and offense and keeping within the boundaries of the four corners is the heart of sil lim tao. Any style which blocks and attacks simultaneously will be structurally faster than a style which incorporates a block and then an attack. The Chinese call the simultaneous block and attack lin sil die dar.

Figures 1 through 4 show the wasted movements that I am expending to counter my opponent's technique. This is not an example of lin sil die dar.

(1) Never use this block in wing chun. It violates the boundary line by passing the shoulder. (2) A palm-up block is a more economical way to defend your outside high gate.

(3) This low block is too extreme—too much wasted motion. (4) You can defend the same area more economically with a slap block to the low gate.

(5) The right arm is beyond the boundary line of the right upper gate. Too much motion is wasted. (6) An economical block would be a slap block to the high gate. Remember to keep your hand within the boundary line.

(7) The boundary line is again violated. The block is too extreme and the movement is wasted. (8) A low outside wrist block is faster to execute and stays within the boundary line. Notice how the right hand is guarding the centerline (joan sien).

THEORY OF FACING

Since the structure of wing chun is based on straight punches, guarding the centerline, elbow in, and immovable elbow, knowing how to face your opponent (*jiue ying*) is essential.

(1) I am not facing my opponent nose to nose. Consequently, all my opponent has to do is come in at an angle and my centerline is useless.

When I face my opponent (2), I preserve my centerline and make it inviolate. I am able to block my opponent's left punch because I am facing him.

FOOTWORK

Advance

(1) Begin the advancing movement by assuming a right stance. (2) Without changing the position of your arms, take a full stride forward with your right foot, and (3) follow halfway with your left foot.

Retreat

(1) In the retreating movement just reverse the direction of the advance. From the right stance (2) slide your left foot backward, and (3) then bring your right foot back halfway.

Step to the Left

(1) Assume a right stance. (2) Slide your left foot toward the left on a straight line, and (3) follow halfway with your right foot.

Step to the Right

(1) Assume the right stance. (2) Slide your right foot toward the right on a straight line, and (3) follow halfway with your left.

Side Step Right into Left Stance

(1) In this maneuver you begin in a right stance but end in a left stance. (2) Slide your right foot forward and toward the right.

Side Step Left Remaining in Right Stance

(1) Assume a right stance. (2) Move your left foot forward and toward the left until it is on line with the right foot.

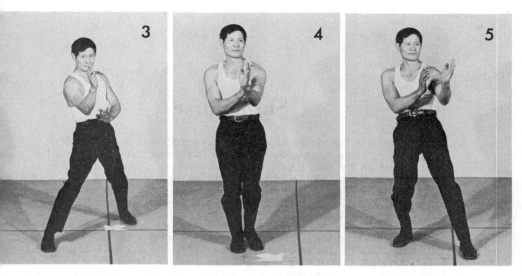

(3) Stop the right foot and follow with your left foot. (4) Without stopping the movement, slide your left foot up to the right foot and (5) then forward and toward the left. This foot movement is used mainly for attacking to both the inside and outside gate.

(3) Bring your right foot over to the left foot, and (4) then slide the right foot forward and toward the right. (5) Follow halfway with your left foot.

Shift Horse

(1) First, assume the square stance with your right hand forward. (2) Shift to a right sitting horse by twisting your body to the right and putting most of your weight on the rear (right) foot. Drop your right hand, palm down, in front of your groin. (3) To attain the left sitting horse stance, shift your weight to your left foot and twist your body to the left. The positions in Photo Nos. 2 and 3 are used to block kicks to the groin area. (4) From the left sitting horse stance slide your right foot to the left foot and (5) then move it backward. Stop the right foot when you are in a left stance. (6) Slide the right foot up to the left foot again and (7) continue to move it forward into a right stance. (8) Bring your right foot back to the left foot, and (9) slide your right foot toward the right into a square stance. Place your left hand forward. The entire sequence of positions, 1 through 9, can be executed in a continuous motion as an exercise.

SIL LIM TAO

Sil lim tao, the first form of wing chun, teaches correct elbow position, protection of centerline, and economy of movements in attack and defense.

Since sil lim tao is a stationary form, you will practice all of your defensive blocks and offensive attacking tools without taking a single step. The hand movements will later be put to good use in the practice of *chi sao* (sticking hands). Sil lim tao is also applied effectively in a combat situation.

Sil lim tao plays such an important part in wing chun training that you should start each practice session with this form before going on to more advanced techniques.

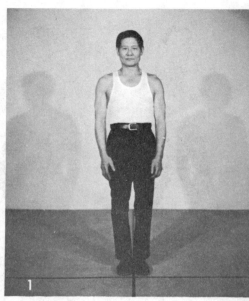

FRONT VIEW

(1) Stand at attention with your feet together and hands at your sides.

SIDE VIEW

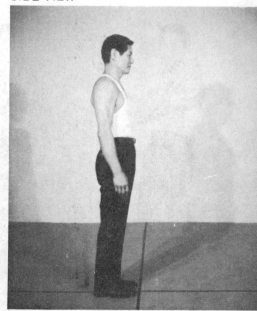

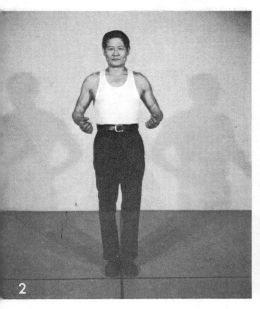 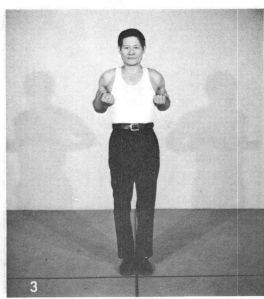

(2) Keeping your body erect, raise your hands. Clench your fists as you turn your palms upward. (3) Stop the fists, palms facing upward, at the pectoral muscles (chest).

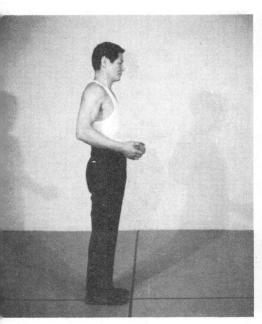 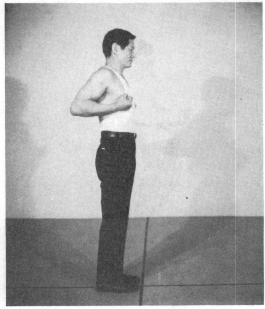

(4) Drop into a half-squat position with your knees together. (5) Simultaneously move the toes of your feet outward without changing the heel position.

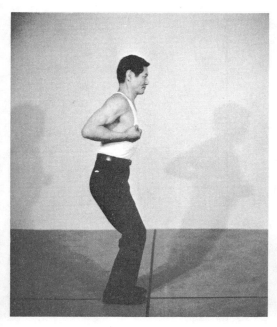

(6) Transfer your weight to the toes and simultaneously move your heels outward. (7) You are now in the bent-knee, pigeon-toe stance (*yee jee kim yang mah*). Maintain this stance throughout sil lim tao.

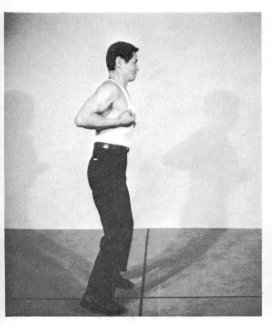 

(8) Bring your hands downward, opening them as you turn the palms toward you. Cross your arms (left over right) at the wrists, in front of your groin, pointing your fingers toward the floor. (9) Without moving your upper arms, raise your hands.

(10) Point your fingers toward the ceiling, and begin to move your hands outward. (11) Again make a fist, bringing your hands to shoulder level. Your palms are still facing you.

(12) Bring your hands straight down to chest level, and turn your palms toward the ceiling. This position is identical to figure No. 7. (13) Begin a left vertical punch toward an imaginary target at nose level. Turn your fist clockwise so the palm is facing to your right. Keep your wrist straight and your elbow in. Intersect the centerline with the punch.

(14) At the conclusion of the punch, your arm should be fully extended and directly in front of your nose. (15) Keeping your arm straight, open your fist and turn your palm toward the ceiling to form a palm-up block (*tan sao*).

(16) Without moving your arm, turn your palm toward your chest, and rotate your hand clockwise to form the circling block (*hieung sao*). (17) Continue to rotate your hand clockwise until your palm faces the floor.

(18) Turn your palm back toward your right and begin to make a fist. (19) As you retract your fist to your chest, turn the palm toward the ceiling.

(20) Continue to retract your fist. (21) With both fists now at your chest, you are in the same position as in figure No. 7.

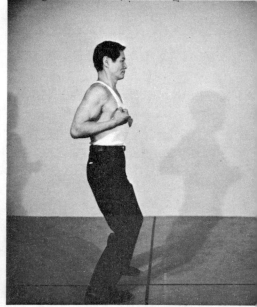

(22) Start to make a right vertical punch to an imaginary target at nose level. Turn your fist so the palm is facing toward your left. Keep your wrist straight and your elbow in. Intersect the centerline with the punch. (23) At the end of the punch, your arm should be fully extended and directly in front of your nose (*jik chung*).

(24) Keeping your arm straight, open your fist and turn your palm toward the ceiling to form a palm-up block (tan sao). (25) Without moving your arm, turn your palm toward your chest, and rotate your hand counterclockwise.

(26) Continue to rotate your hand until the fingers point toward the floor.
(27) Keep your palm facing the floor as you straighten your fingers.

(28) Begin to form your hand into a fist. (29) Turn your palm toward the ceiling as you retract your fist to your chest.

(30) Continue to retract your fist to your chest. (31) With both fists at your chest, you are again in the basic sil lim tao position shown in figure No. 7.

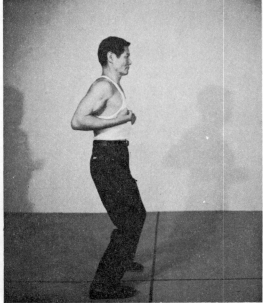

(32) Open your left hand with the palm facing up to form the palm-up block. Begin moving your hand outward from the center of your chest. (33) Extend your arm only three quarters. Do not straighten it.

(34) Turn your palm toward you with your fingers pointing toward your chest. (35) Begin to rotate your hand clockwise.

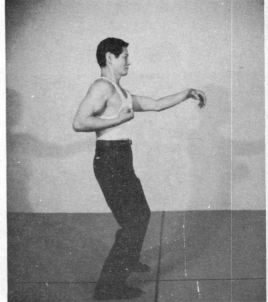

(36) Stop the rotating movement when the thumb is pointing toward you and the palm is facing to the right. (37) Pull your hand toward you, but don't touch your body with the left elbow.

(38) Relax your wrist and point your fingers toward your chest. Keeping your elbow tucked in during the forward motion, extend your left arm. (39) Rotate your hand clockwise.

(40) At the end of the rotating movement, your thumb should be toward your chest. Face your palm to the right. (41) Retract your left arm until your elbow is about three inches from your body.

(42) Relax your wrist, pointing your fingers toward your chest. In order to develop *fook sao* (the "elbow in" bent block), movements 38 through 42 should be repeated three times before going on to 43. (43) Stop the movement of your wrist when the thumb faces toward you and the palm faces toward the right.

(44) To execute the *pak sao* (left slap block), move your hand to the right—but not past the right shoulder—, with your thumb toward you and your palm facing right. (45) Return your hand to the middle of your chest.

(46) Push your left hand outward to an area directly in front of your nose (*yun jeong*). Extend your arm completely, and turn your palm away from your chest, (47) rotating it toward the ceiling to form tan sao (palm-up block).

(48) Begin to rotate your hand in a clockwise motion again. (49) When your palm faces the floor, start to make a fist.

(50) With the palm up, begin to bring the left fist back to your body. (51) Stop the movement when your fist reaches the left side of your chest in the basic sil lim tao position shown in figure No. 7.

(52) Open your right hand with the palm facing up, forming the palm-up block. Begin moving your hand outward from the center of your chest. (53) Extend your arm only three quarters. Do not straighten it.

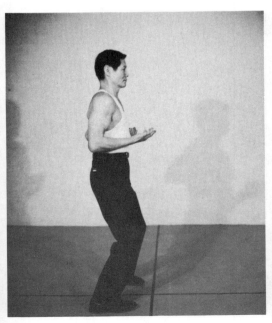 

(54) Rotate your hand counterclockwise, with your fingers pointing toward your chest. (55) Keep the elbows stationary as you continue the rotating movement.

(56) Stop the rotating movement when the thumb points toward your chest and the palm faces to the left. (57) Bring your right elbow to within three inches of your body.

(58) Relax your wrist. (59) Keep the elbow in toward your body during every forward motion. With the wrist still relaxed, begin to straighten your arm until it is about three quarters extended.

(60) Keeping the elbow in place, start rotating your hand counterclockwise.
(61) Stop the rotating movement with the thumb facing your chest and the palm facing toward the left.

(62) Bring the elbow back to within three inches of your body. (63) Repeat the sequence in figures 58 through 61 three times before going on to 64.

(64) Perform a right-hand slap block to the left. Remember not to go past the left shoulder. (65) Return your hand to the middle of your chest.

(66) Execute the vertical palm strike by extending your arm, with the palm facing away from you, to an area directly in front of your nose. (67) Turn your palm up to form tan sao (palm-up block).

(68) Rotate your hand counterclockwise without moving your arm or elbow.
(69) When your palm faces the floor, begin to form a fist.

(70) Retract your fist to (71) the right side of your chest, in the basic sil lim tao position.

(72) With the left hand, begin a palm strike toward the floor. (73) Open your hand and extend your arm.

 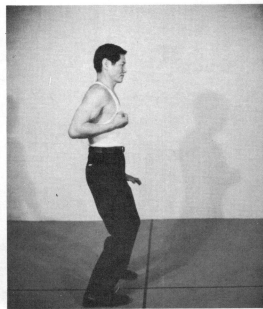

(74) Begin a right palm strike toward the floor. (75) Both arms are now fully extended and both palms are facing the floor.

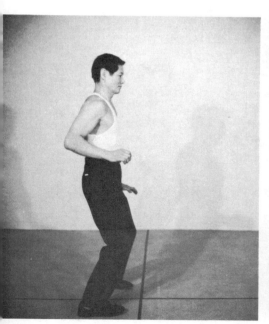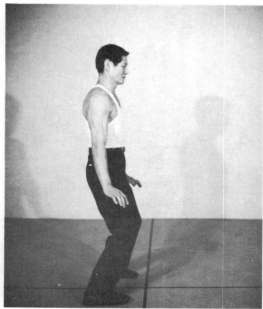

(76) Lift both hands, palms down, to waist level and toward the rear. (77) Execute a double palm strike to the rear.

(78) Raise your hands and bring them to the front at about chest level. (79) Execute a double palm strike in front of your groin.

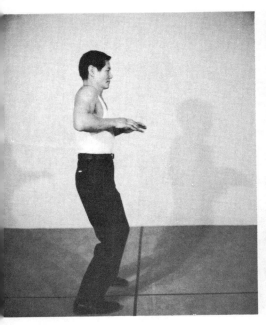

(80) Lift both hands and begin to cross the left over the right. (81) Raise the left arm to shoulder level and hold the right arm below and parallel to the left. The palms are faced toward the floor.

(82)Simultaneously swing both arms out, and extend them to your sides in *sol jee* (outside sweep or sweeping fingers). (83) Return your arms to the original position (an inside eye sweep) in front of your chest. This time, place the right arm above the left.

(84) To execute a sinking elbow block, raise both forearms so they are parallel, with the palms facing each other. (85) Without moving the elbows, execute a palm-up block (tan sao) by turning the two palms up.

(86) Turn the palms away from you and jerk them downward (*jut sao*). (87) Quickly extend both hands in a double jab to the eye (*bil jee*).

(88) After executing the finger jab, drop both arms, palms down, in front of your groin in defense against a groin kick. (89) Still extended, move your arms up, with the palms facing you and fingers pointing toward the floor.

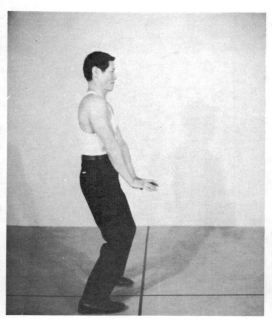 

(90) Form your hands into fists as you retract them to your chest. (91) Turn the palms up so that you are again in the basic sil lim tao position.

(92) Perform the left slapping block (pak sao) to the right, but do not move your hand past the right shoulder. (93) Return your hand to the middle of your chest, keeping the elbow three inches from your body and the fingers pointed toward the ceiling.

(94) Execute a left, sideward palm strike (*woang jeong*) by thrusting your palm straight out at face level. (95) Then rotate your hand to the palm-up position.

(96) Rotate your left hand in a clockwise motion. (97) Make a fist and begin to return your arm to your side.

(98) Turn your palm toward the ceiling as you continue to retract your hand to your chest. (99) Both palms face up in the basic sil lim tao position.

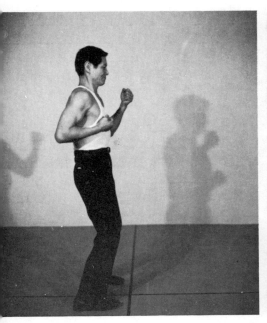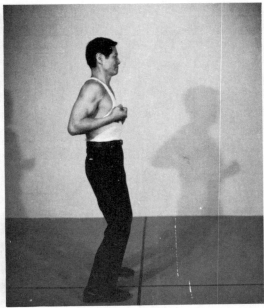

(100) Execute a slap block to the left, but do not pass the left shoulder with your hand. (101) Return your hand to the center of your chest.

(102) Execute a sideward palm strike with your right hand. (103) Turn your palm toward the ceiling to form a palm-up block.

(104) Begin to rotate your hand in a counterclockwise motion. (105) At the end of the rotating movement, start to form a fist and retract your arm.

(106) Continue retracting your arm until (107) your fist reaches the chest in the basic sil lim tao position.

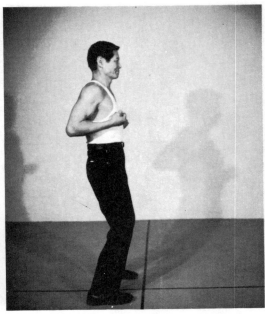

(108) Starting from the centerline, form a palm-up block. (109) Extend your arm three quarters.

(110) Without bending your arm, change to a low block (*goang sao*) by turning your palm toward the floor, straightening your arm, and lowering your hand to waist level. (111) Return your arm to the palm-up block.

(112) Rotate your hand clockwise, (113) stopping your hand when it is in the side palm strike position.

 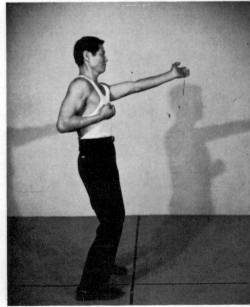

(114) Turn your hand to the palm-up position and (115) continue to rotate your hand clockwise.

116

117

(116) Begin to form a fist and turn the palm upward. (117) Retract your hand to your chest with the palm up.

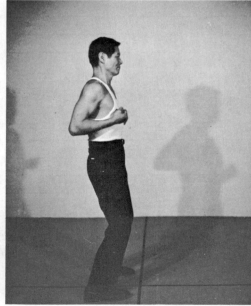

(118) Assume the basic sil lim tao position. (119) Extend your right arm three quarters to form the palm-up block.

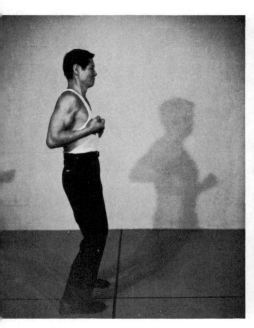

(120) Turn the palm downward, lowering your arm as you fully extend it to form a low block. (121) Return your arm to the palm-up block.

(122) Without moving your elbow, rotate your hand counterclockwise. (123) Begin a sideward palm strike.

(124) Fully extend your arm to complete the sideward palm strike. (125) Form your hand into a fist and begin to retract it to your chest.

(126) Stop your fist on the right side of your chest in the basic sil lim tao position. (127) Begin the elbow-up block (*bong sao*) by raising your elbow until your forearm is parallel to the floor. This is the only block in which your elbow is raised.

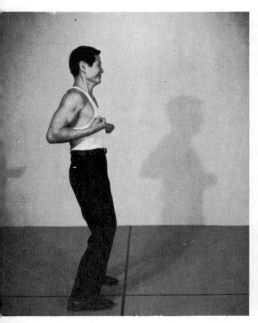

(128) Complete the elbow-up block by moving your arm—your hand open—diagonally across your chest. (129) From the elbow-up block bend your elbow and turn your palm toward you in sinking elbow block (*chum jiang*).

(130) With your elbow still bent, start the palm strike (*dia jeong*) by bending your fingers downward so that your palm is facing the ceiling. (131) Complete the palm strike by fully extending your arm at face level.

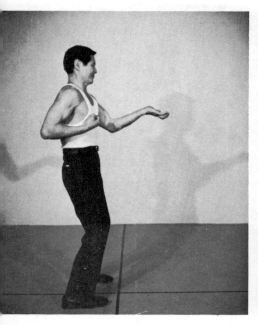 

(132) Begin to rotate your hand clockwise, with your palm toward your body. (133) Start to retract your hand and make a fist.

(134) Return your left fist to the side of your chest. (135) With the palm facing up, you are in the basic sil lim tao position once more.

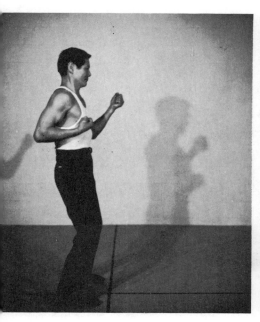
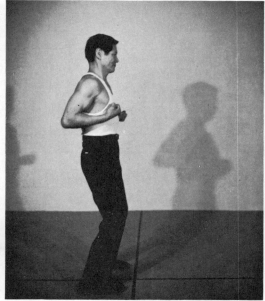

(136) Begin the elbow-up block with the right arm. (137) Complete the block by lowering your forearm diagonally across the chest.

(138) From the elbow-up block, drop your elbow into a sinking elbow block, and (139) begin the downward palm strike.

(140) Complete the palm strike with your arm extended and your hand at face level. (141) Rotate your hand counterclockwise until your palm faces your body.

(142) Form a fist with your right hand as you begin to retract it toward your body. (143) Continue retracting your fist to the right side of your chest.

(144) Stop your fist, with the palm up, next to your chest. (145) Slant your left arm across your body with the palm facing the floor.

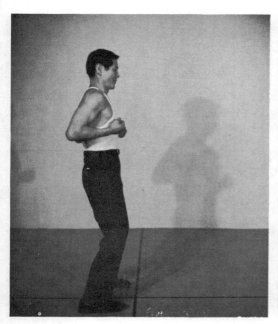

(146) Bring your right hand, palm facing left, to the middle of your chest. (147) Cross your right arm over the left, simultaneously retracting your left hand to your side as you form a fist.

(148) After the right arm completes a slicing movement across your body, your fist should be palm-up at your side. (149) With your left hand, shoot out a vertical punch at nose level as your right fist protects your chest.

(150) Then shoot out a right vertical punch at nose level and retract the left arm. (151) Repeat the left-right punches three times before going on to movement No. 152.

(152) After completion of the last punch, thrust the right arm up into a palm-up block. (153) Begin to rotate your hand counterclockwise until the palm faces toward your chest.

(154) Form a fist and retract your hand until (155) it is at the side of your chest.

 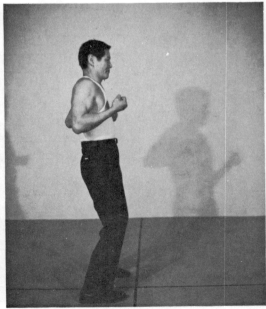

(156) From the basic sil lim tao position, (157) slide your left foot over to your right foot. Stand erect with your feet together.

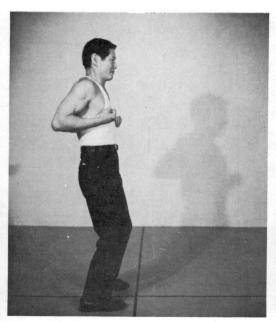 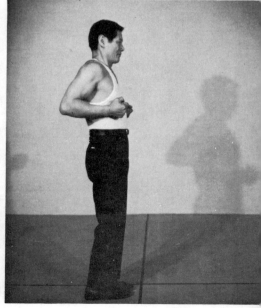

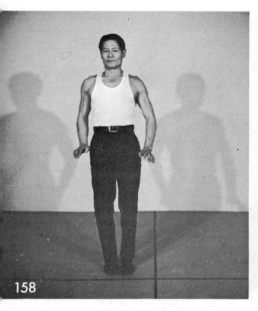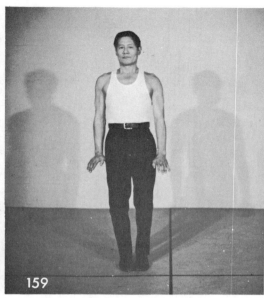

(158) Open your hands and rotate the palms downward, moving them along the thighs. (159) With the arms extended, palms facing the floor, and feet together, you have returned to the starting position of this form.

Note: In the beginning of sil lim tao both feet are together and on the cross line. At the completion of sil lim tao both feet are together and to the side of the cross line.

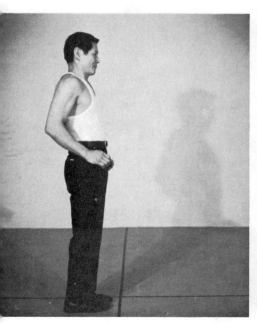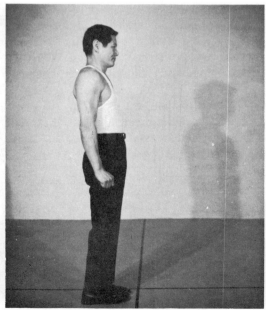

STRAIGHT PUNCH and FINGER JAB

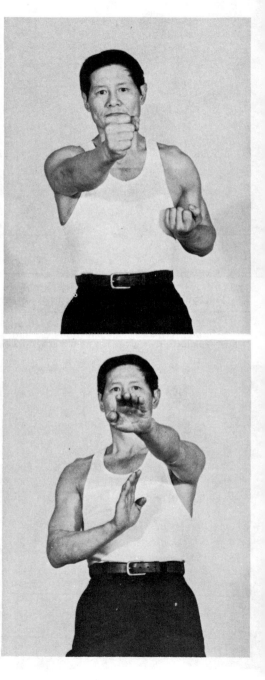

Wing chun attacking weapons are simple and direct—mainly straight punch and vertical fist. A jab or punch can be of two types: inside gate or outside gate.

In the traditional classical wing chun kung-fu, these weapons are used most frequently: straight punch, finger jab, finger sweep, vertical palm, sideward palm, downward palm, straight kick, and side downward kick.

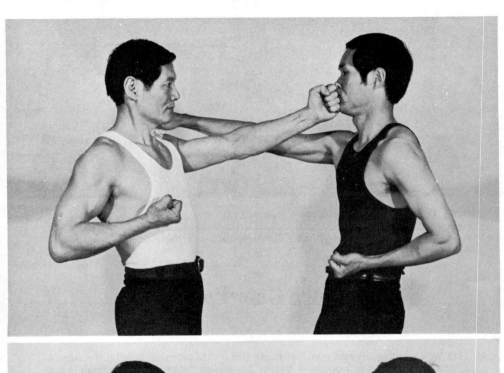

(A) To execute the inside gate punch (*noy moon chuie*), assume the basic square stance. (B) Start the punch from the middle of your chest, and (C) extend your arm so that your hand intersects the centerline.

Inner Gate Punch

(1) When facing an opponent, execute the inside gate punch from the square stance. (2) As your opponent begins his punch from the waist, begin your punch from the middle of your chest. (3) Make sure your arm goes to the inside of your opponent's arm. (4) Strike your opponent in the face while blocking his punch with your striking arm. (5) As you withdraw your right arm, begin a left inside gate punch. (6) Execute the left inside gate punch as you did the right. (7) Deflect your opponent's blow with your striking arm. A finger jab can be used in the same way.

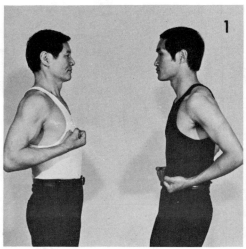
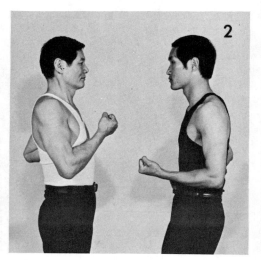

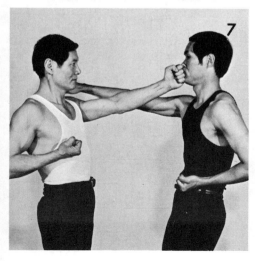

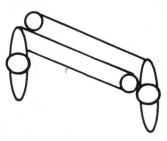

The top view of the inside gate punch clearly shows how your opponent's punch is deflected. The attacking hand is also the blocking hand.

(A) Begin the outside gate punch by first assuming the basic square stance. (B) Start your punch from the side of your chest, and (C) intersect the centerline with your fist.

Outer Gate Punch

(1) When facing an opponent, execute the outside gate punch from the square stance. (2) As your opponent starts his punch from the waist, start your punch from the side of your chest. (3) In this case your arm goes outside of your opponent's arm. (4) Strike your opponent in the face while forcing his punch inward and away from your face. (5) Withdraw your right arm and start a left outside gate punch. (6) The inside of your left elbow begins to deflect your opponent's punch at this point. (7) Strike your opponent's face at nose level.

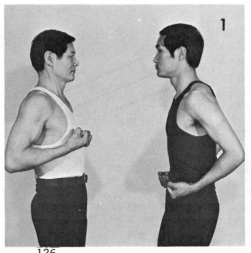

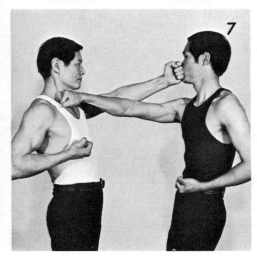

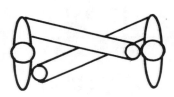

The top view of the outer gate punch block shows how you deflect your opponent's punch inward.

KICKS

Although wing chun puts more emphasis on hand techniques than kicking, there are two kicks that are frequently used in this kung-fu style: the front thrust kick and the downward side kick.

High Straight Kick

(1) To advance into the high straight thrust kick, assume a right stance. (2) Stride forward with your right foot. (3) Bring your left foot up to your right, and (4) kick with your right foot to face level.

**FRONT VIEW
FINAL POSITION**

**FRONT VIEW
FINAL POSITION**

Middle Straight Kick

(1) To advance to the middle straight thrust kick, again assume a right stance. (2) Stride forward with your right foot. (3) Bring your left foot up to the right foot, and (4) kick with the right to groin level.

Downward Side Kick

(1) To advance into the side kick, assume a right stance. (2) Stride forward with your right foot. (3) Bring your left foot up to the right foot. (4) Raise your right knee to

**FRONT VIEW
FINAL POSITION**

waist level. (5) Pivoting on your left foot, turn your right side toward your opponent, and kick out at about knee level with the side of your right foot.

The wing chun kick can be used both for attacking and for obstructing an opponent's kick as shown in the following pages.

Application

(1) To apply a straight thrust kick against an opponent, assume a right stance. (2) Stay in that position as the opponent begins to advance. (3) As your opponent kicks

with his right foot, begin an inside low gate block with your left hand. (4) Raise your left knee as you block the kick with your left hand, and (5) deliver a straight left thrust kick to the groin.

Application

(1) If you move in to press an attack without kicking, chances are you will be open for a kick from your opponent. (2) Use the wing chun downward side kick as an obstruction. (3) Then it will be safe to advance and attack. Notice how the opponent's right arm and leg are checked as the straight punch (jik chung) is thrown.

Application

(1) Prepare to receive a right kick by (2) using your right foot to block your opponent's kick. (3) Shift to a left stance and throw a straight left punch, checking your opponent's right leg with your left leg.

Application

(1) If your opponent lunges forward, (2) remain ready in a right stance. (3) When he steps down to deliver his punch, counter with a fake finger jab as you unleash a right straight kick to the groin.

Application

(1) Attempt a right finger jab. (2) If your opponent blocks the jab and attacks with a right punch, (3) change to a right grabbing hand (lop sao) and slide your left foot up to your right foot. (4) Jerk your opponent's right arm downward with your right hand and execute a straight, right thrust kick to the groin. Make sure your left hand is held high and your right hand is held low.

SIMULTANEOUS
ATTACK and DEFENSE

Any practice in which you block and then hit is structurally slow. A physically fast man will never attain full realization of his aim in a structurally slow style. The object of wing chun, a structurally fast style, is to develop physical speed. It teaches the use of offense as defense. If you sense that your opponent is going to throw a hook to your face, beat him to the punch with a finger jab.

A. A strip of paper that's black on one side and white on the other can be used to explain the concept of lin sil die dar. The white stands for a block, and the black stands for an attack.

B. This stands for a structurally slow style. The black and white don't merge.

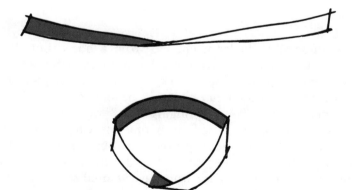

C. By twisting the paper, black runs into white and white runs into black. Block and attack become one, representing a structurally fast style.

CHI SAO
(STICKING HANDS)

It is impossible to learn chi sao from a book, but it is even worse to try to learn this form by self-experimentation. Self-practice will only develop a jerky, up and down, left to right wrestling contest which can be easily penetrated by a sharp wing chun practitioner. The "springing out" of constant, forward energy can only be acquired from practice with an experienced teacher—it can never be captured on film or paper. Chi sao demonstrations have been filmed and run in slow motion by instructors from other styles who have wanted to learn the secret. Alas! All they could copy were the arm movements.

Chi sao is not a method of fighting. It is a method of developing sensitivity in the arms so you can feel your opponent's intentions and moves. Chi sao teaches correct elbow position, the right type of energy, feeling for an opponent's emptiness, and defending with minimum motion by keeping within the nucleus of

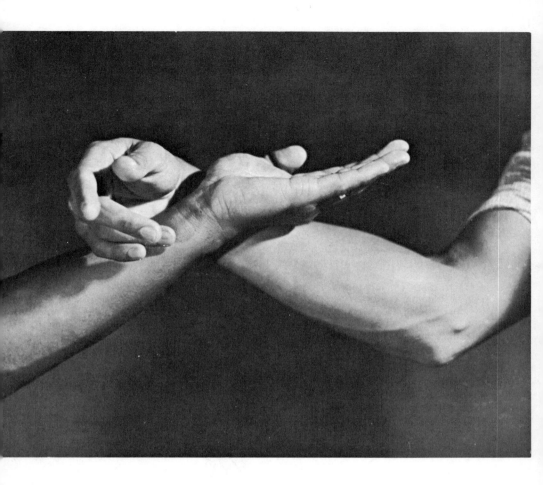

the four corners. Movement in chi sao is like a flowing stream—never still. It avoids the "clinging stage" (the mind stopping to abide) and the attaching of one's self to a particular object rather than flowing from one object to another. If you set yourself against an opponent, your mind will be carried away by him. Don't think of victory or of yourself.

My emphasis has been on the constant flow of energy. Such energy should not be misinterpreted as being a secret, mysterious, or internal power. The primary approach to chi sao practice is to hone technical skill to a razor's edge for instinctive hand placement so basic in the wing chun style. The better and more constant your flow (which is only developed by sticking hands with a competent teacher), the more you can take advantage of the opponent's most minute openings.

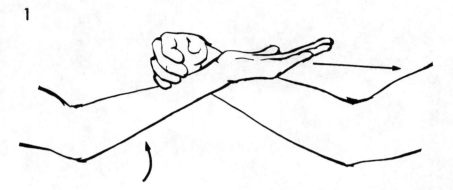

(1) In *doan chi sao* the two opponents face each other in sil lim tao's basic bent-knee-pigeon-toed-half-squat position. (You should not move from this stance during sticking hand practice.) To begin, the person on the left extends his arm in a palm-up block. The person to the right puts his right arm on top of his opponent's left arm in a bent-arm, elbow-in block (fook sao).

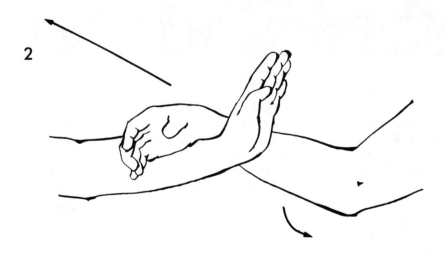

(2) Left uses the palm-up block to open up his opponent's centerline so he can strike with a vertical palm (yun jeong). The person on the right "feels" his opponent's vertical palm and goes into an elbow-in block by dropping his elbow downward and inward to deflect the vertical palm.

3

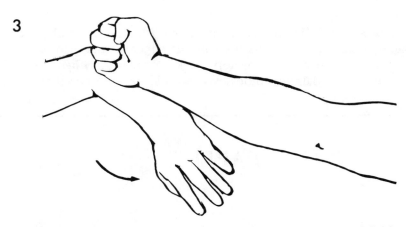

(3) From the elbow-in block, the man on the right tries a vertical fist toward his opponent's face. The man on the left "feels" the vertical fist attempt and goes from a vertical palm to an elbow-up block, which deflects the straight punch.

4

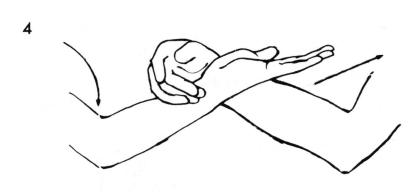

(4) The hands return to the original positions, with the person on the left extending his arm in a palm-up block and the person on the right putting his right arm on top of his opponent's. The arms are touching throughout the exercise. (In practice, repeat this procedure several times.)

In essence, the sticking hands practice is like the Oriental game of paper, scissors, rock. Scissors can cut paper, a rock can crush scissors, and paper can envelop rock. Similarly, when your opponent uses a palm-up block, you should execute an elbow-in

PAPER

ROCK

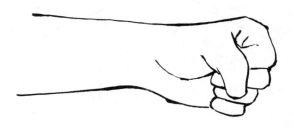

block. When your opponent strikes from the elbow-in block, change to an elbow-up block. The one who can't change effortlessly will be defeated.

SCISSORS

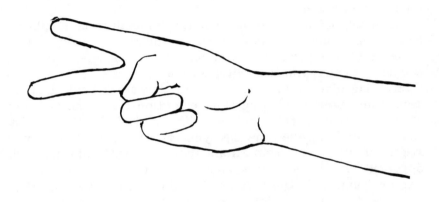

PAPER

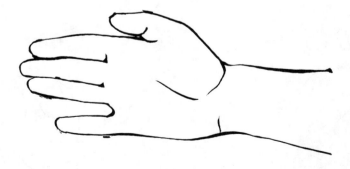

TRAPPING HANDS

Immobilizing an opponent's hands in wing chun is called *phon sao*. Literally translated, phon means to seal or to close off an object or area. However, the English word immobilize is probably the best translation of phon.

If, in self-defense, you momentarily immobilize an assailant's hands, his ability to defend or counterattack is decreased tremendously, especially if you immobilize his legs, too. In a couple of seconds you can deliver the coup de grace.

Still, ingenious as the techniques are, they are difficult to apply against an experienced wing chun practitioner and can be more effectively used against people who like to block and then hit. By carefully studying the drawings, you can see how the beginning stages of phon sao start from the opponent's block. If an opponent blocks and strikes simultaneously, it is not so easy to trap his hands, although it can still be done with correct practice.

Since the ability to trap hands depends to a large extent on sticking hands—skill and sensitivity which can only come by learning from experienced wing chun practitioners—, it would be very dangerous to try these techniques against a wing chun man, especially if you are self-taught.

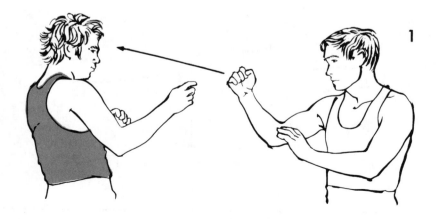

1

(1-2) Strike with a right straight punch toward your opponent's face. If your opponent uses a right palm-up block against your punch, (3) grab his right wrist with your right hand and jerk his arm downward as you punch with a left fist. If your opponent blocks your left punch, (4) cross grab his left wrist with your left hand and pull it across his body as you execute a right punch to the face. Use your opponent's left arm to immobilize his right arm. Make sure, too, that you immobilize your opponent's leg with your leg.

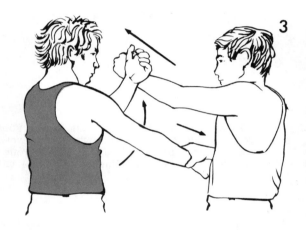

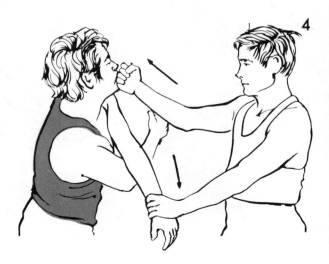

(1) Lead with a right straight punch inside your opponent's left guard. (2) As your opponent blocks your right arm downward, prepare to execute a left grabbing hand to his left wrist. (3) Grab your opponent's left wrist and jerk his arm down as you attack to the face with a right back fist. If your

3

opponent blocks your back fist with his right arm, (4) cross grab his right wrist with your right hand and jerk his arm downward and across his body as you deliver a straight left punch. Use your opponent's right arm to immoblize his left arm.

4

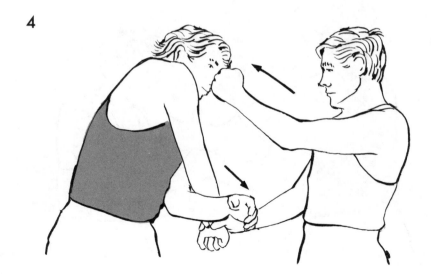

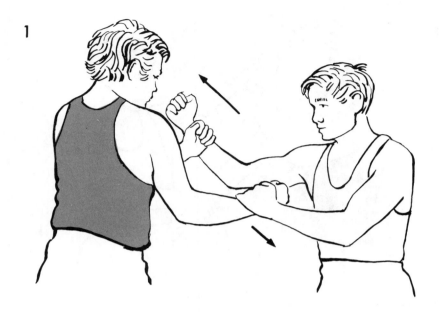

(1) Punch with your right fist as you grab your opponent's right wrist with your left hand. (2) If your opponent blocks your right punch with a left palm-up block, (3) execute a double jerk by grabbing his left blocking hand

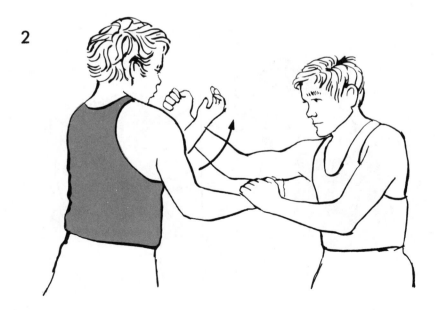

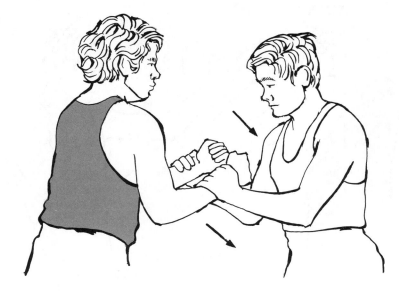

at the wrist and pulling it down to the level of his right hand. (4) From the jerking hands, cross your left hand over and grab your opponent's left wrist as you release your grip with the right and then punch with the right.

4

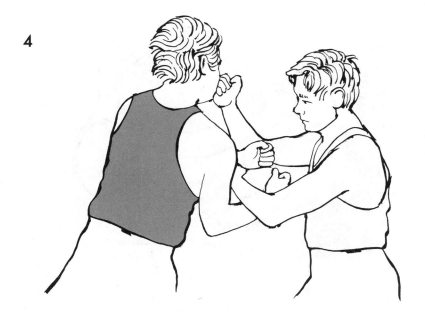

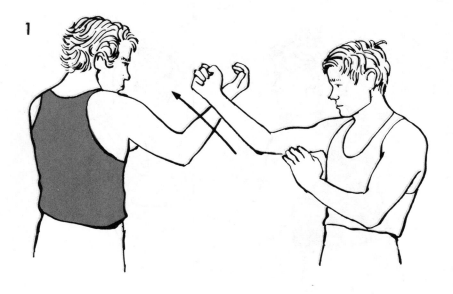

(1) Lead with a straight right punch. If your opponent blocks your punch with a right palm-up block, (2) grab his right wrist with your right hand and jerk it down as you punch with a straight left. If your opponent executes a left slap block against your left punch, (3) change the punch to a left palm-down press and immobilize both of his arms by pushing his left hand

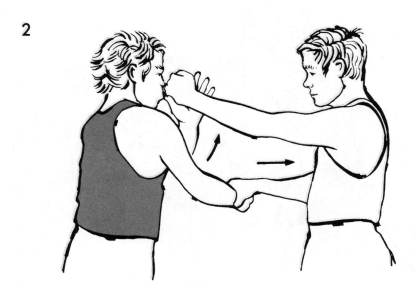

3

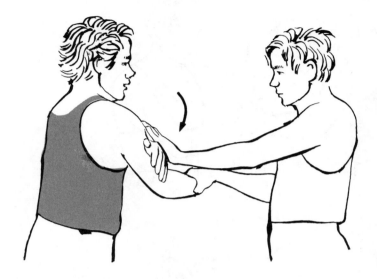

against his right arm. (4) Continue to hold your opponent's left hand down with your left hand as you punch with the right fist. You can switch and also press with your right hand and strike with the left fist. In any event, your opponent's arms will remain immobilized.

4

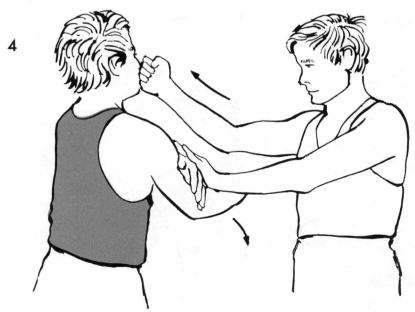

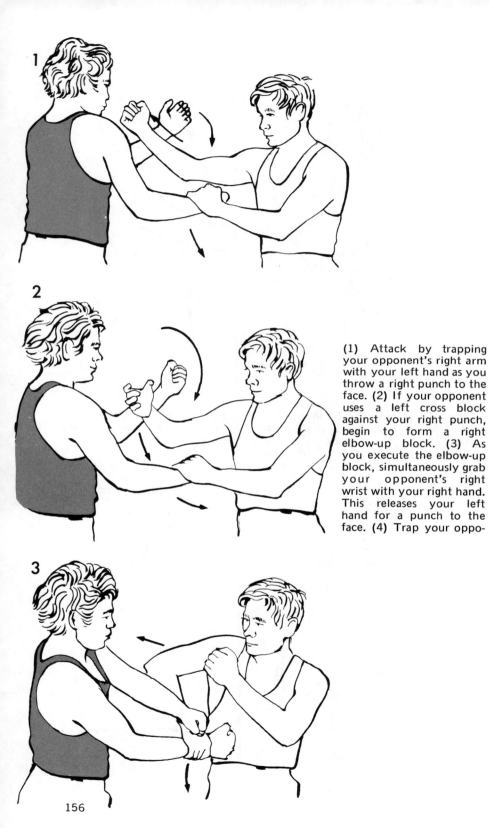

(1) Attack by trapping your opponent's right arm with your left hand as you throw a right punch to the face. (2) If your opponent uses a left cross block against your right punch, begin to form a right elbow-up block. (3) As you execute the elbow-up block, simultaneously grab your opponent's right wrist with your right hand. This releases your left hand for a punch to the face. (4) Trap your oppo-

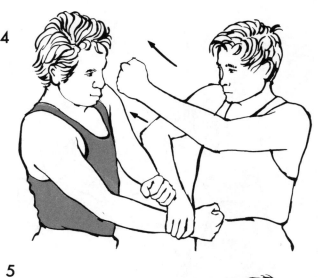

4

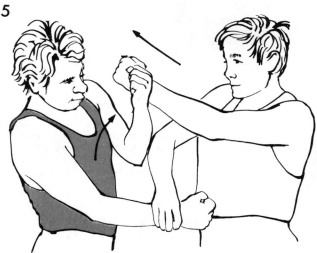

5

nent's left arm with your right arm as you strike to the face with a left straight punch. (5) If your opponent slips the elbow-up block and blocks your left punch with his left arm, (6) execute a left cross grab to his left wrist and pull his left arm down across his body and over his right arm, using his left arm to trap his right arm as you execute a right back fist.

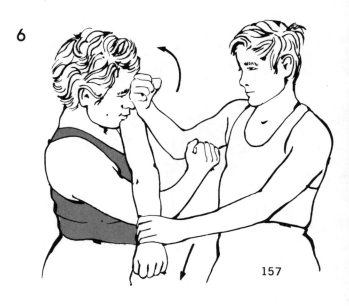

6

(1) This immobilizing technique takes perfect timing and a great deal of practice. When your opponent attacks with a straight right punch, respond with a right palm-up block. (2) If your opponent grabs your right wrist with his right hand as he punches with the left,

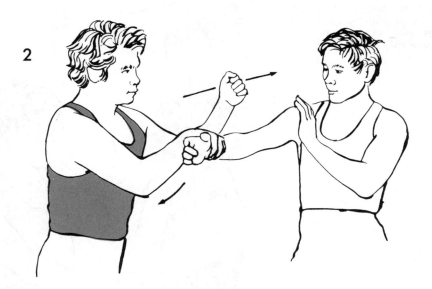

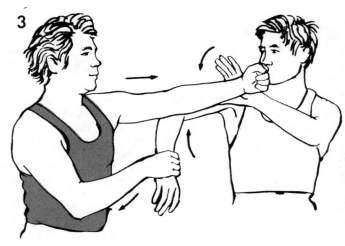

3

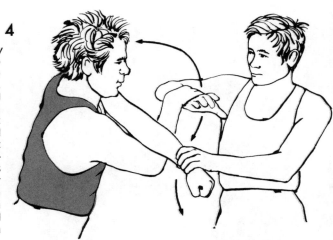

4

(3) counter the blow by changing your right arm to an elbow-up block to deflect the left punch. Begin a grabbing hand with your left hand. (4) Grab your opponent's left wrist with your left hand and try to execute a right back fist. If your opponent's right-hand grip is too strong, (5) grab your opponent's left wrist with your right hand as you release your left grip and punch to the face with a left fist.

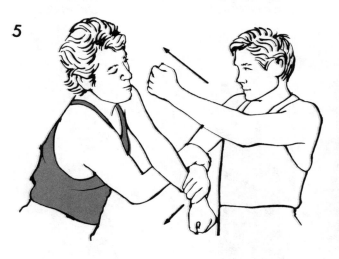

5

PARRIES

The success of wing chun in a counterattack is due to the technique of momentarily trapping and immobilizing your opponent's hand, making it much easier, quicker, and safer for you to deliver a barrage of blows.

Combinations of counter blows are usually delivered from the grabbing hand (*lop sao*) and the slapping block (*pak sao*). The variations of the grabbing hand are the inside grab (*noy lop*) and the outside grab (*gnoy lop*). The variations of the slapping block are the inside slap (*noy pak*) and the outside slap (*gnoy pak*). There is also a cross grab block and a cross slap block.

When your opponent's hand is on top of your arm and is pushing your arm across your body, use the elbow-up block to pin and immobilize his arm.

Grab and Strike

(1-2) If your opponent uses a left palm-up block against your right punch, (3) simply change to a right elbow-up block (bong sao). (4) Begin to execute a left grabbing

hand by (5) grabbing your opponent's left wrist and jerking his arm downward as you deliver a right back fist to the temple.

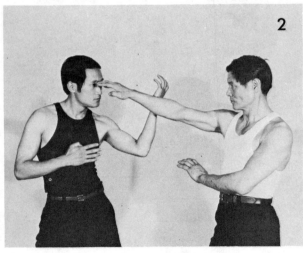

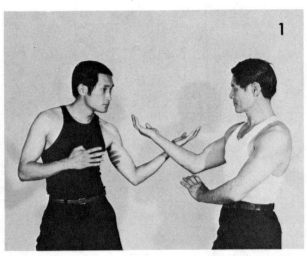

Block and Strike

(1) Execute a right palm-up block to expose your opponent's centerline, then (2) use the same hand for a finger jab to the eyes. You can follow up with a series of finger jabs or vertical fists. (3) If your opponent tries to force

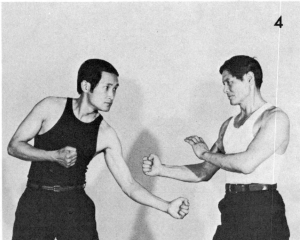

your right arm downward, (4) simply circle your hand counterclockwise and (5) execute a right vertical fist to the face. This is an example of a running hand and strike (*jull dar*). Follow up with a left punch or a finger jab.

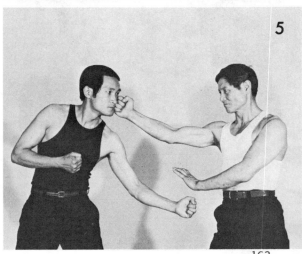

Jerk
and Strike

(1) When your opponent's left hand is under your right, (2) trap and strike with the same hand by first jerking his right hand downward and then (3) executing a

right vertical fist. (4) If your opponent's right hand is under your left, (5) you can jerk his right arm down with your left hand and simultaneously strike with your right.

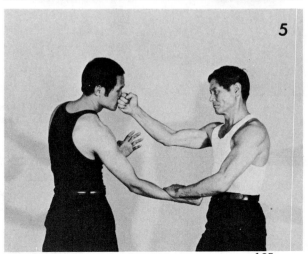

Outside Grab

(1) When your forward arm is on the outside of your opponent's, use the outside grabbing hand (lop sao) by (2) grabbing your opponent's right arm with your right hand and jerking it down as you execute a left vertical fist.

Inside Grab

(1) The second grabbing technique, inside grabbing hand (inside lop), is used when your forward arm is on the inside of your opponent's arm. (2) Grab your opponent's right wrist with your forward (left) hand and jerk his arm downward as you execute a right vertical fist to the face with the free (right) hand.

Cross Grab

(1) Use the cross grab (cross lop) when your forward arm is on the inside of your opponent's and he tries a palm-up block. (2) Simply slip your left arm underneath your right arm and (3) grab your opponent's left arm with your left hand. (4) Jerk his arm down as you deliver a right back fist.

Outside
Slap and Strike

(1-2) After you execute a right slap block to your opponent's right hand, begin to follow with a left slap block. (3) Execute the left slap block to your opponent's right arm as you strike with a right vertical fist to his face.

Inside
Slap and Strike

(1) As your opponent begins to shoot out a left jab, (2) begin to execute a left, cross slap block (3) as you throw a right vertical fist.

DEFENDING
THE INSIDE GATES

This chapter illustrates how to put the lin sil die dar concept to practical use by using the basic blocks from sil lim tao.

Defending
Inside Low

(1-2) If your opponent begins a right lunge punch after feinting with a high left hand, wait as long as possible before you (3) simultaneously execute a left slap block (pak sao) and a right vertical fist (jik chung).

Defending Inside Low

(1) If your opponent is in a left stance and (2) kicks to your inside low gate with his right foot, (3) execute a right slap block to his kicking leg and shift your horse to the right side. (4) As your opponent with-

draws his foot, begin to slide your right foot toward your left foot. (5) Change into a left stance and attack with a simultaneous left palm to the face and a right downward palm to the groin (double palm strike).

Defending Inside Low

(1-2) As your opponent begins a right punch from a left stance to your inside gate, (3) simultaneously execute a left, low outer wrist block (goang sao) and a right vertical fist.

Defending
Inside Low

(1-2) If your opponent changes to a right stance in executing a right lunge punch, (3) simultaneously execute a left, low outer wrist block and a right vertical fist.

Defending Inside Low

(1-2) As your opponent begins a right corkscrew punch, (3) simultaneously execute a left slap block and right vertical fist.

Defending Inside Low

(1) Assume a right stance if your opponent is in a twist horse stance. (2) If he attempts a left punch that's out of range, raise your left hand to block but don't attack. (3) As your opponent twists right and attempts a right hook to your solar plexus, (4) simultaneously execute a left slap block and a right vertical punch.

Defending
Inside Low

(1) If your opponent attempts a right hook to your body, (2) wait as long as you can before (3) simultaneously executing a left slap block and a right vertical fist.

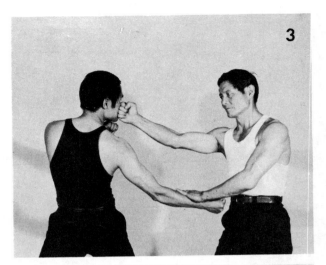

(4) If your opponent withdraws his right fist and starts a left punch, (5) use minimum motion to simultaneously execute a right, palm-up block and a left vertical fist.

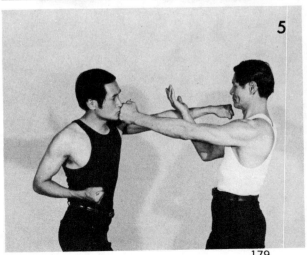

Defending Inside High

There are many ways to defend against multiple attacks. By practicing sil lim tao with its primary blocks, you should be able to spontaneously execute the blocks in any situation. This series of photos shows a combination defense against an opponent's right and left attacks. (1-2) When your opponent tries a right

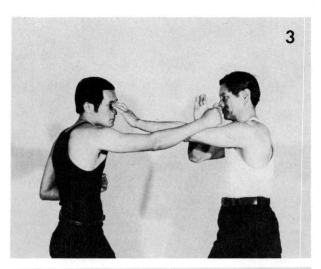

punch to your face, execute a right, cross slap block (3) as you shoot out a left finger jab to his eyes. (4) If your opponent then withdraws his right hand and attempts a left punch to the body, (5) use minimum movement in simultaneously executing a left cross slap block and a right finger jab.

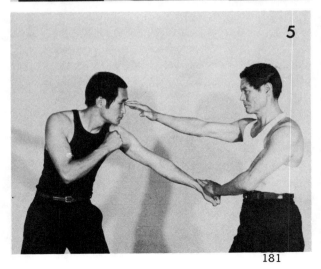

Defending Inside High

(1-2) If your opponent tries a hook kick, execute a left palm block. (3) When his foot comes down, simultaneously check his elbow with your left hand and punch with your right.

Defending
Inside High

(1) If your opponent is in a twist horse stance and (2) begins spinning left with a back fist, (3) simultaneously execute a left palm-up block and a right vertical fist. (4) Then simultaneously grab your opponent's wrist with your left hand and his elbow with your right hand, pulling his arm down as you execute a side kick to the side of the knee. You can follow with a right back fist or a left punch to the head.

Defending Inside High

(1-2) As your opponent attempts a right punch, (3) simultaneously execute a left palm-up block and a right vertical fist. (4) If your opponent withdraws his right hand and begins a left hook to

the body, (5) drop your right hand into a low, outer wrist block as you throw a left vertical fist. In this case you drop from an inside, high gate defense into a low, outside gate defense.

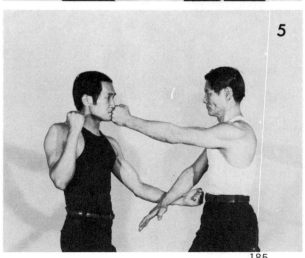

Defending Inside High

(1-2) If your opponent attempts a right punch to your inside high gate, (3) cross your right hand over for a simultaneous right slap block and a left finger jab.

Defending Inside High

(1-2) As your opponent attempts a right punch to your inside high gate, (3) shift to a right sitting horse and simultaneously execute a left palm-up block and a right vertical fist.

Defending Inside High

(1-2) If your opponent attempts a right blow to your inside high gate, (3) use your left hand to block. (4) Then if he

pulls his right hand back and attempts a left punch, (5) simultaneously execute a left slap block and a right back fist.

DEFENDING
THE OUTSIDE GATES

Defending Outside Low

(1-2) If your opponent lunges toward you and steps down to deliver a right punch to your outside low gate, use a right, low outer wrist block. (3) Then raise your right arm out of the wrist block (4) and execute a left slap block as you simultaneously deliver a right back fist to your opponent's temple. A more economical alternative would be to skip the low outer wrist block in Photo No. 2 and go straight to the techniques of Photo Nos. 3 and 4.

Defending
Outside Low

(1) Don't be disturbed if your opponent assumes a classical stance. Stay in a right stance. (2) If he advances with his left foot and (3) attacks with a left hand, drop your right elbow to block the strike (chum jiang). (4) Then immediately attack with a left back fist.

Defending Outside High

(1-2) If your opponent attempts a left jab to your head, (3) use your right hand to block and attack simultaneously. Keep your left hand up for double safety in case your opponent's strike slips in. Whenever possible, use the simultaneous block and strike (*lin sil die dar*).

Defending Outside High

(1-2) As your opponent shoots out a left jab, (3) simultaneously execute a left, cross slap block and a right punch to the solar plexus. (4) If he withdraws his left hand and

starts a right blow, (5)
shift into a right sitting
horse stance and simulta-
neously execute a left
palm-up block and attack
to the face with a right
finger jab.

Defending Outside High

(1-2) As your opponent shoots out a straight right, (3) execute a right, outside palm-up block. (4) If he withdraws his

right hand and begins a left hook, (5) waste no motion in executing a left slap block and a right back fist.

Defending Outside High

(1-2) If your opponent attempts a left jab to your face, (3) use a simultaneous left, cross slap block and a right finger jab. (4) If he with-

draws his left fist and attempts a right hook to the stomach, (5) drop your right hand into a cross slap block as you strike with a left vertical fist.

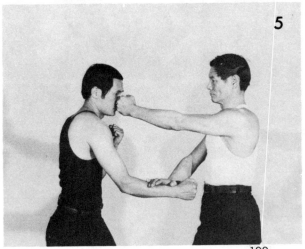

ATTACKING THE INSIDE and OUTSIDE GATES

Attack
Outside High

(1-2) Begin a right finger jab to your opponent's outside high gate. If he blocks your attack with his right hand, (3) change the finger jab to a grabbing hand (outside lop sao), simultaneously jerking your opponent's right arm downward and delivering a left vertical fist to the head. Be cer-

tain that you also immobilize your opponent's right leg with your right leg. (4) Check your opponent's right elbow with your left forearm, and then (5) press his right arm back with your left hand so there is no chance for a counter. Punch to the face with a right vertical fist.

Attack Outside High

(1-2) Advance your right leg, preparing to attack with a finger jab. (3) Attack to your opponent's outside high gate as you check his front foot with your front foot to keep him from kicking.

Attack
Outside High

(1) From a right stance (2) advance with a right low feint and begin trapping your opponent's right leg. (3) When your opponent attempts a low block against your right feint, (4) raise your right arm and begin a left slap block. (5) Simultaneously deliver a right back fist and a left slap block. You can follow with a left punch or finger jab.

Attack Outside Low

(1-2) Attack with a straight left punch. (3) If you feel resistance from your opponent's right hand, (3) immediately change your left punch into a left slap block as you deliver a right punch to the solar plexus.

Attack
Outside Low

(1-2) Advance your left foot up to the right foot and kick with a right, middle straight thrust kick.

Attack Inside High

(1) From the right stance (2) slide your right foot forward and to the right. (3) Then bring your left foot forward as you begin to execute a left palm-up block. (4) Continue to move your left foot toward your opponent. When you are in a left stance, simultaneously execute a left palm-up block and right vertical fist.

Attack
Inside High

(1-2) Advance from a right stance and begin a left jerking hand. Immobilize your opponent's right foot with your right foot. (3) Jerk your opponent's right arm down with your left hand as you execute a right vertical fist.

1

2

Attack Inside High

(1-2) From the right stance, slide your right foot forward and to the right, using your left hand to guard against a kick. (3) Bring your left foot up to the right foot. (4) Move your left foot

3

forward into a left stance as you execute a left palm-up block and a right punch. (5) As you retract your right hand, punch with your left. (6) Retract your left hand and follow up with another right punch.

1

2

Attack Inside High

(1-2) Advance your right foot forward to attack from a right stance. (3) Execute a left slap block to your opponent's right forearm as you attack with a straight, right vertical fist. (4) If your opponent blocks your right with his left hand,

3

(5) begin a left cross grab (*lin lop*) to his left wrist as you prepare to execute a right back fist. (6) Deliver a right back fist to the face as you pull your opponent's arm across his body. Notice that the opponent's arms and left leg are immobilized.

Attack
Inside Low

(1) From a right stance (2) feint with a right finger jab. (3) Bring your left foot up to your right foot and lower your right hand to block against the kick. (4) Simultaneously execute a left slap block and kick to your opponent's groin with your right foot.

Attack
Inside Low

(1) From the right stance (2) feint a finger jab with your right hand, then (3) quickly lower it to guard against a kick as you bring your rear (left) foot up to your right foot. (4) Stride forward with your right foot, (5) slapping your opponent's right elbow with your left hand as you punch to his stomach with your right.

Attack
Inside Low

(1) From a right stance (2) stride forward with your right foot, feinting with a right finger jab. (3) Follow with your left foot. (4) Use a right obstruction kick to guard against a kick from your opponent as you advance. (5) If you deliver a low right blow and your opponent blocks it, (6) slip past the block with a running hand (*jull sao*). (7) From the running hand deliver a right vertical fist to your opponent's jaw as you jerk his right hand downward with your left.

TRAINING METHODS

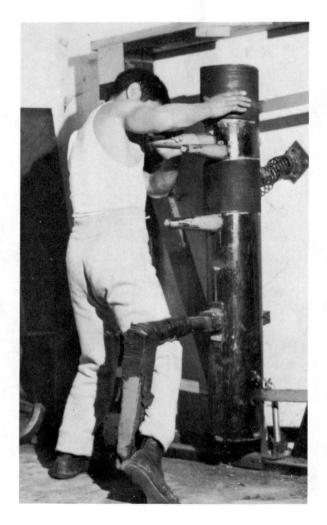

There are many training methods used in sharpening the execution of the various wing chun techniques. One hundred and eight techniques can be performed against the wooden dummy, the most sophisticated wing chun training device. A sand bag, even a piece of paper or a handkerchief are also effective training devices. If you have a partner, you can use him to practice many of the same techniques that are performed against the dummy.

CIRCLING-WRIST EXCERCISE

You'll recall that in the first form, sil lim tao, there are many wrist circling movements. These wrist movements are mainly used when your hand is on top of your opponent's and you execute the circling-wrist block (hieung sao). The best way to practice the circling-wrist block (other than with a competent instructor) is with a wooden dummy.

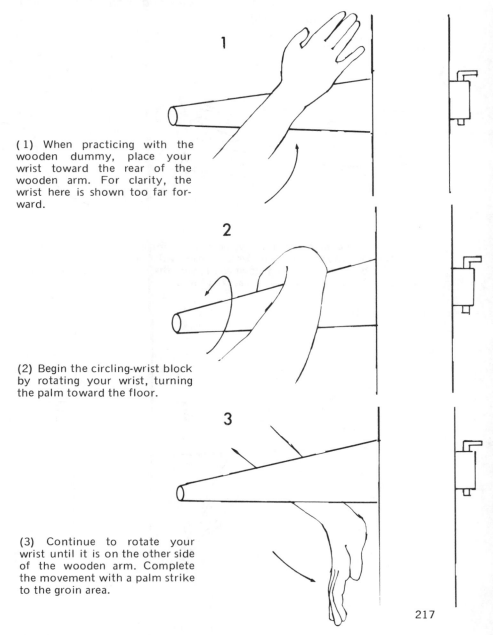

(1) When practicing with the wooden dummy, place your wrist toward the rear of the wooden arm. For clarity, the wrist here is shown too far forward.

(2) Begin the circling-wrist block by rotating your wrist, turning the palm toward the floor.

(3) Continue to rotate your wrist until it is on the other side of the wooden arm. Complete the movement with a palm strike to the groin area.

EXERCISES FOR
STRENGTHENING THE BRIDGE

Your blocking hand, "bridge", is only as effective as your ability to withstand a hard blow from an opponent. Although it's more desirable to deflect a strike rather than taking the full force of the blow on your forearm, it is sometimes unavoidable in a fast exchange. Here are a few exercises (with and without a partner) used in strengthening the bridge.

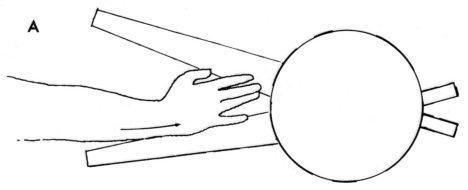

A. When working with the dummy, go straight for the dummy's centerline and bump the wooden arm with your outside wrist area. B. Strengthen the outer wrist block by blocking downward with the edge of your wrist. All movements should be repeated at least ten times.

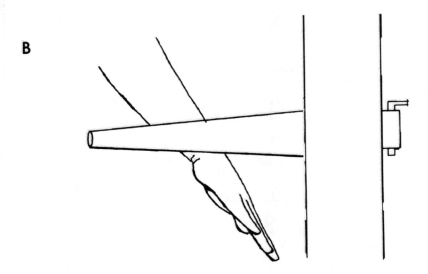

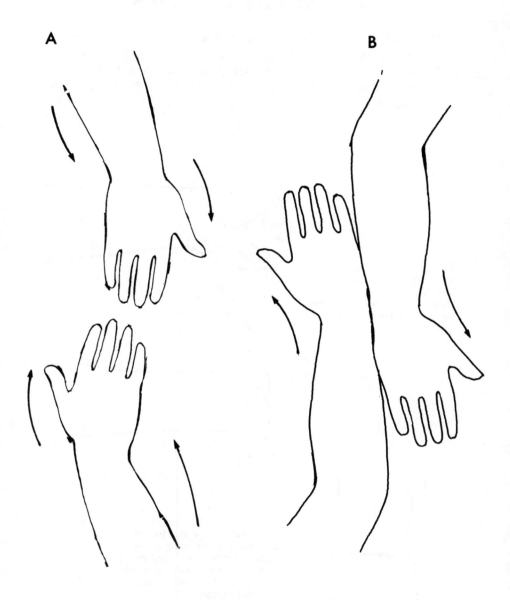

A. Begin the exercise for strengthening the bridge by facing your opponent. Use your right arm with your hand pointing to the right. B. At the moment of impact, turn your hand slightly to the left. Execute ten repetitions before switching to the left hand.

PUNCHING EXERCISES

The wing chun sand bag is circular and is mounted against a wall at about chest level. Its use is to develop strength in the wrist for the vertical fist. Practice the punch from the square, right and left stances. Some wing chun practitioners prefer dry peas in the bag instead of sand.

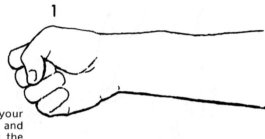

(1) Before striking, bend your wrist slightly downward and keep the fist loose. (2) At the moment of impact, the wrist is straight and the fist is tight.

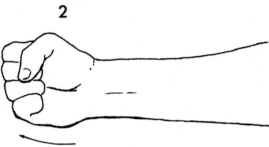

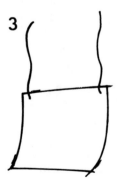

(3) Another way to practice punching is to hang a piece of paper from the ceiling and punch at the paper. Instead of paper, a light, silk handkerchief can also be used.

CHINESE TERMINOLOGY IN KUNG-FU

bi jong . . . . on-guard stance

bil jee . . . . finger jab

bil jee . . . . "flying fingers" (3rd wing chun form)

bong sao . . . . elbow-up-in-air block

cheong . . . . spear

cheong kil lik . . . . long bridge strength

chum jiang . . . . drop-elbow block

chum kil . . . . . "searching for the bridge" (2nd wing chun form)

die jeong . . . . downward palm strike

ding sao . . . . bent-elbow-forward-energy block

do . . . . knife or sword

don chi . . . . single sticking hand

fa kune . . . . flowery hands, ineffective style

fook dar . . . . attacking from the bent-arm block

fook sao . . . . bent-arm-elbow-in block

gim . . . . sword

gnoy lop . . . . outside grab

gnoy pak . . . . outside slap block

goang sao . . . . low outer wrist block

go dar . . . . high blow

gong . . . . hard

har dar . . . . low blow

hieung sao . . . . circling-wrist block

jee yao bok gik . . . . free style

jik chung, chung chui . . . . vertical fist

jik tek . . . . straight kick

joan dar . . . . middle blow

jong sao . . . . 108 techniques on dummy

jor mah . . . . sitting horse stance

juk tek . . . . side kick

jull dar . . . . running hand and strike

jull mah . . . . running the horse

jull sao . . . . running hand

jut sao . . . . jerking hand

kok soot . . . . national art

kwon . . . . staff

kwoon . . . . school, gym, institute

ling wood . . . . fast and accurate

lin lop . . . . cross grab

lop sao . . . . grabbing hand

mah . . . . horse stance

mo hay . . . . kung-fu weapons

mook jong . . . . wooden dummy

noy moon chuie . . . . inside gate punch

noy pak . . . . inside slap block

noy sing . . . . patience, perseverance

nuie toe . . . . female student

pak dar . . . . attacking from the slap block pak sao . . . . slap block

qua chuie* . . . . back fist

sao fot . . . . hand techniques

seong chi . . . . double sticking hand

si bak . . . . instructor's senior

si dai . . . . one who learned after you, your junior

si fu . . . . instructor

si gung . . . . grandfather, your instructor's teacher

si hing . . . . . one who learned before you, your senior or brother

si jo . . . . founder of the style

sil lim tao . . . . "little imagination" (1st wing chun form)

si sook . . . . instructor's junior

tan dar . . . . attacking from the palm-up block

tan sao . . . . palm-up block

toe dai . . . . students

toe suen . . . . student's student (grandchildren)

woang jeong . . . . sideward palm strike

yee kim yang mah . . . . pigeon-toed stance

yuen . . . . soft

yun jeong . . . . vertical palm strike

* Qua chuie (back fist) is not used in the traditional or classical teaching of wing chun. My use of the back fist in the techniques in this book is a result of my instructor's influence on me in my early training. Instead of the back fist, a classical practitioner would use the vertical fist.

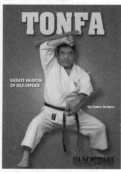

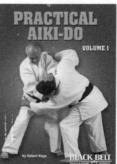
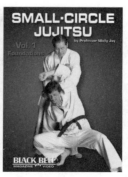